THE KEA

A collection of photographs by **Corey Mosen**
and information collated by the **Kea Conservation Trust**

Published 2014

by **BOOKS**

ISBN 978-0-9941070-9-1

Printed by The Copy Press, Nelson, New Zealand.
 www.copypress.co.nz

This book is a collection of photographs by Corey Mosen as well as information collated by the Kea Conservation Trust to bring to light the beauty, joys and hardships faced by the kea (Nestor notabilis) in New Zealand.

For more information:
www.coreymosen.co.nz
www.keaconservation.co.nz

Kea are a unique and endangered parrot
endemic to the Southern Alps of New Zealand.

Kea are the only alpine parrot species in the world and now number fewer than 5,000 individuals in the wild.

Kea are highly gregarious, forming large social flocks in the wild with non-linear hierarchies.

The kea is a strong flier with a wing span of over a metre.

Viewed from beneath, the underwings of the kea are a striking orange-red with black and yellow striped primary feathers. Rare sightings of yellow or albino kea have also been recorded.

Both male and female kea are predominately olive green with black trim around the edge of their feathers, with some iridescent blue feathers allowing for camouflage in the wild.

Male kea are up to twenty per cent larger than females and can be identified by their larger, prominently hooked upper mandible.

Juvenile kea can be differentiated from adults through a distinctive yellow coloration around their eyes, mandible, and nostrils (cere), which gradually fades to grey/black by about four years of age.

Kea have been known to live up to fifty years in captivity
and more than thirty years in the wild.

The key to the kea's survival is its ability to adapt
to its changing environment and exploit a variety of
food resources as they become available.

Kea are predominantly vegetarian, opportunistic feeders, although some have been seen feeding on sea-bird chicks, insects and lizards.

Once adult kea reach breeding age at around three to
four years of age they tend to leave the main flock,
then pair up for breeding and raising of chicks.

Kea nest on the ground, usually in rock cavities but sometimes in a hollow tree or under roots.

Unfortunately it is a common occurrence that kea nests are predated during the nesting season, usually by introduced pest species such as stoats and possums.

Kea have a long nesting period and it takes around four months for chicks to fledge.

Kea have an extended juvenile period and are dependent
on their parents for up to six months.

The environment the kea live in is extremely harsh and variable. Kea have evolved to cope with the associated survival pressures this environment presents.

The habitat of the kea extends from South Island beech forests to alpine meadows and mountain scree slopes.

Kea are known to be important in the dispersal of a huge variety of alpine plants.

Kea are often seen around mountain passes and at ski fields. They are well known for destroying window wipers on cars and for stealing the belongings of campers.

The kea's intelligence and natural curiosity continues to cause conflict with people who live in or utilise the South Island alpine areas.

Kea are extremely adaptive and are considered to be one of the most intelligent bird species in the world.

There is a population of kea in Vienna, Austria, that have been studied extensively and are being taught to use a touch screen computer to communicate.

There is evidence to show that kea are able make use
of natural tools to gather food.

Starvation, predation, ingesting rubbish, and direct human interference are the greatest causes of death of kea in the wild.

Lead poisoning is a real problem for kea in the wild. It was once a common building material and still persists on old buildings in kea habitats. It disrupts the reproductive cycle, causes cognitive problems and in severe cases can result in death.

Numbers of kea were substantially reduced in the past
with the introduction of a bounty. This resulted in over 150,000
birds being culled, continuing as late as the 1970s.

Kea are now listed as a nationally endangered species and the future of the wild kea population remains precarious.

Work continues with monitoring the remaining wild kea population to ensure numbers are stable, as well as developing techniques to minimise kea damage to human property.

From a young age, Corey Mosen has been intrigued by animals. This curiosity has led to him earning a degree in zoology, doing voluntary work with sea turtles on a Greek island, working with monkeys at a zoo, studying endangered owls at the Grand Canyon, and working with kiwi, kokako and lizards in the North Island for the Department of Conservation. He has also worked on animal research projects in Australia and Mozambique. More recently his work has taken him to the mountains of the South Island, working on various kea projects for DOC and the Kea Conservation Trust. Corey's passion for photography goes hand in hand with his dream job.